W9-CAH-679

<u>practical guidelines</u>

Family Life Education in Multicultural Classrooms

Nancy Abbey
Claire Brindis, DrPH
Manuel Casas, PhD

Ana Consuelo Matiella, MA, Editor

ETR Associates
Santa Cruz, California
1990

This book was made possible by a grant from The General Service Foundation, St. Paul, Minnesota, 1986.

© 1990 ETR Associates.
Published by ETR Associates,
P.O. Box 1830, Santa Cruz, CA 95061-1830
To order call toll-free 1-800-321-4407

Printed in the United States of America
10 9 8 7 6 5 4 3 2
Title No. 590
Design by Julia Chiapella

Library of Congress Cataloging-in-Publication Data

Abbey, Nancy, 1933-
   Family life education in multicultural classrooms: practical guidelines /
Nancy Abbey, Claire Brindis, and Manuel Casas; Ana Consuelo
Matiella, Editor.
      p. cm.
   Includes bibliographical references (p.)
   ISBN 1-56071-025-X
   1. Family life education—Study and teaching—United States.
2. Multicultural education—United States. I. Brindis, Claire D. II. Casas,
Manuel. III. Matiella, Ana Consuelo. IV. Title.
HQ10.5.U6A23   1990
306.85' 07—dc20   90-39224

Dedication

This guide is respectfully dedicated
to the ETR Associates Training Department.

Table of Contents

Preface

The original work for this guide was made possible by a grant from The General Service Foundation. The guide was conceived by the staff of ETR Associates in response to a question asked by family life educators throughout the United States: "How can family life education be made more culturally and ethnically relevant and appropriate in the multicultural classroom?"

This work began in 1986, under the guidance of an outstanding advisory committee made up of ten family life and sex education professionals. With the helpful suggestions of many other educators in California and throughout the United States, we have brought together information, guidelines and suggested teaching approaches.

These approaches and guidelines were refined by several other working committees of educators from various cultural and ethnic backgrounds. We hope this work will prove valuable to the many family life educators whose real concern and caring led them to ask the question.

Readers of this guide should realize that cultural and ethnic traditions, beliefs and values are affected by individual life experiences, including gender, occupation, income, place of birth and role models. Bicultural students live both within their cultural framework and outside of it. Multicultural students integrate several cultures: class, neighborhood, ethnicity and the youth culture of the United States.

Although this work represents many hours of collective thinking, discussion and refinement, it is clearly only a first step. We hope that this first step will begin an ongoing dialogue that will strengthen the commitment to make family life education relevant to all students in our schools.

In the true spirit of dialogue, we would like to encourage you as readers and educators to write to us at ETR Associates. We welcome your comments and suggestions on how family life education can better serve the wonderful diversity of our student population and our nation.

Please address your comments to:
Ana C. Matiella, Editor
ETR Associates
P.O. Box 1830
Santa Cruz, CA 95061-1830

Acknowledgments

The authors and ETR Associates wish to thank the advisory committee members for the knowledge, experience and insight they have contributed to this project and for their sheer vitality, humor and enthusiasm, which made the advisory committee meetings inspiring and enjoyable.

Advisory Committee

Lisa Correa-Mickel
Wilma Espinoza
Patricia Gómez-Lopp
Debra Hansen-Arce
Susana Hennessey
Louis Hernández

Wilma Montañez
Alida Pastoriza-Maldonado
Edgar Quiroz
Concepción Tadeo
Jerry Tello

We would like to give special thanks to the ETR Associates Training Department and the Multicultural Guidelines Advisory Committee for their work on and refinement of the guidelines.

Training Department Staff

Hector Campos
Cherri Felder
Elizabeth Raptis Picco

Multicultural Guidelines Advisory Committee

Janet Collins
Lisa Correa-Mickel
Brother Joseph Desimone
Pat Gacoscos
Karen Gee
Dong Hau
Father Bill Johnson

Donzella Lee
Lorena Martinez
Maria Natera
Pam Rector
Julie Van Putten
Susan Varner
Mical Visher

Introduction

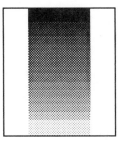

Why This Guide Is Important

F or years educators have been struggling with the question of how to make education appropriate and relevant in the multi-cultural classroom. Poor academic performance, high drop-out rates and the under-representation of so-called minorities in the professions attest to the difficulties our educational system has had in responding to the needs of our ethnically diverse student population.

The face of America and American schools is rapidly changing. Our schools must serve increasing numbers of students from diverse cultural and ethnic backgrounds. In the year 2000, minority enrollment in U.S. school systems is expected to exceed 35%, according to the U.S. Department of Education.

Birth and immigration trends indicate that members of the White mainstream population are having fewer children. Soon the term *minority* will be a misnomer. In California, for example, it already is.

There, a more accurate term is the *emergent majority*. Students from diverse cultural and ethnic backgrounds, including Latinos, Asians and Blacks, made up 51% of the student population in 1988-1989. This number is expected to continue to rise.

There is no doubt: We are a pluralistic nation. The increasingly challenging task that we have before us as educators is to educate *all* our children.

So Why Is This Guide Important, Really?

In the setting of family life education, active socialization takes place, and social information is given out. As we examine the topics of family life education, we realize that all teaching occurs in a sociocultural context. All educational materials have the potential to reflect social values.

This guide is important for the following reasons:

• We sharpen students' understanding of our society in our schools.

• Teachers are powerful transmitters of culture.

• Our educational system is the great socializer.

• The hope for our educational future is in a culturally pluralistic nation that accepts and prepares all citizens to be worthwhile contributors.

This guide is also important because all aspects of family life education have the potential to promote interpersonal as well as intergroup awareness. Very simply put, family life education is an ideal place for our children to learn about life.

Multicultural education—or at least, multicultural relevancy in education—offers both children and teachers an opportunity to grow and understand themselves and each other.

We have said it in the Preface, and it merits repeating here: this guide is a first step in identifying and recommending ways to make family life education more relevant to all students in our educational system. That, too, is why this guide is important.

What Is Family Life Education?

In this guide, family life education is defined as an educational course that provides individuals with adequate and accurate knowledge of family life in its physical, psychological and socio-cultural dimensions.

In its broadest definition, family life education enhances self-esteem and encourages self-understanding; increases skills in decision making and communication; clarifies personal values; promotes respect for family values and the values of others; encourages communication in the family; and promotes fulfilling, healthy and responsible behavior.

What You Will Find in This Guide

F amily Life Education in Multicultural Classrooms presents approaches and guidelines for developing culturally appropriate and relevant family life education. Although the focus of this guide is on family life education, the authors believe that the suggested approaches and recommended guidelines can be applied to all areas of the school curriculum to address the needs of a culturally and ethnically diverse student population.

The guide begins with a definition of culture and a look at different types of acculturation. This section offers educators a sensitivity filter, enabling them to view students and their needs in perspective and with greater understanding.

A section on Cultural Relevance in Family Life Education briefly explains the challenge of a multicultural approach in family life education and offers some initial recommendations.

Acknowledging that self-esteem is a key element in family life education, the section on self-esteem provides an explanation of the Clemes and Bean Theory of Self-Esteem, with a discussion of its multicultural application.

The next two sections provide specific guidelines in outline form. Guidelines for Teachers are provided to help educators develop and teach family life education classes that are sensitive to and reflective of the cultural and ethnic diversity of the students in the classroom.

The Guidelines for School Districts and Decision Makers were developed in the broader context of improving educational opportunities for students. They are directed to school administrators, state boards of education and departments of education.

Under Special Sections, you will find some additional tools specifically addressed to the classroom educator. Checking Out Your Biases is a list of questions intended as a private self-assessment. Curriculum Guidelines for Multicultural Classrooms is a list of pertinent questions that will help you assess the responsiveness of your curriculum to the multicultural needs of students and the diversity of society at large.

Four sample lessons from the *Latino Family Life Education Curriculum Series* exemplify the application of the Clemes and Bean Theory of Self-Esteem. Although the content of the *Latino Family Life Education Curriculum* was developed with the specific needs of Latino students in mind, the process is one that can be used across cultures. The curriculum can be easily adapted to the needs of the multicultural classroom.

The concepts and suggestions in this guide are designed to be integrated into an existing family life education curriculum. We have also provided a list of resources. If no family life education curriculum is in place, these resources might be used as models to be adapted to local needs and standards or as springboards for ideas to develop new programs.

When you are planning a responsive family life education program, we strongly advocate the inclusion of a local advisory committee that is reflective of the community and has active parent involvement.

Family Life Education in Multicultural Classrooms

# What Is Culture?

C ulture can be defined as the body of learned beliefs, traditions, principles and guides for behavior that are shared among members of a particular group. Culture serves as a road map for both perceiving and interacting with the world. Because culture is dynamic and ever changing, the road map can lead in different directions. Culture is a strong determinant of behavior, beliefs, attitudes and values.

People can belong to more than one group at any one time and can possess multicultural attributes. For example, a person born in the United States of Portuguese ancestry might follow, to varying degrees, the national American culture as well as certain aspects of the Portuguese culture. In addition, this person may also be affected by specific regional cultural values. Our cultural attributes are determined by the degree of emotional ties to our respective cultures as well as by factors such as the ethnic makeup of the group in which we interact.

According to cultural anthropologists, universal beliefs, values and behaviors develop because every society provides a blueprint for living. This blueprint includes approved and sanctioned ways to deal with universal circumstances, such as the existence of two sexes; the helplessness of infants; the need for satisfaction of the basic requirements for food, shelter and sex; the presence of people of varying ages; and physical or other capabilities.

If the essential cultures of diverse groups are to survive and endure over time, they must have an element of stability. But they must also have the ability to evolve to meet changing environmental and situational demands. Culture is not a static phenomenon; it is dynamic and everchanging.

We embrace and maintain specific cultural beliefs and traditions because we have been habituated to them through our their upbringing and education. Formally, the enculturation process can be perceived as the result of the teaching of these norms by the older generation to the younger.

However, the enculturation process in general is much broader. In the case of recently immigrated Hispanics, for example, adjustment to or acceptance of the prevailing norms requires that children learn from their parents and that parents and children learn from their peers. But often, because the children have more contact with the majority culture than their parents do, parents learn from their children (Mead, 1970). Due to language barriers, the children of recent immigrants often serve as the link—the spokespersons—between the family and society as a whole.

Acculturation (Social Science Research Council, 1954) is a model of enculturation that can help us understand the adjustments ethnic groups make as they become part of American society. Acculturation is a process that requires contact with at least two autonomous cultural groups. In addition, change must occur in one of the two groups as a result of the contact.

Four types of acculturation that have received attention in social science literature are assimilation, integration, rejection and deculturation.

Assimilation occurs when individuals or groups are willing to relinquish their cultural identity and assume the cultural attributes of a designated group—generally the dominant or majority group. Sometimes, the majority group may also relinquish certain attributes. More often than not, however, the minority group melts into the mainstream culture. When this occurs, the outcome is described as a melting pot.

Integration, in contrast to assimilation, occurs when individuals or groups seek to maintain their cultural integrity while still taking selective steps to become part of the larger society. Integration can enable individuals to develop a bicultural existence that allows them to enjoy the best of both cultures.

Rejection occurs when an individual or a group refuses to assimilate or integrate and instead chooses to withdraw from the dominant culture. The need to maintain the indigenous culture assumes priority over other cultural concerns.

Deculturation occurs when individuals or groups find themselves out of cultural and psychological contact with either their indigenous culture or the dominant culture. Those most likely to be in a state of deculturation are second-generation individuals whose parents fail to or are unable to provide a strong background reflecting their indigenous culture, and those who have not been able to access the mainstream culture and become a part of it.

At the same time, these individuals may create and/or encounter barriers (e.g., associations limited to persons who are similarly self-isolating, segregation policies, ineffective schooling, etc.) that impede their assimilation or integration into the dominant culture. Deculturation as described here constitutes the classic situation labeled by sociologists as *marginality* (Stonequist, 1935).

The acculturation process does not follow a unidirectional continuum. As a result of numerous factors, the direction of the process can be reversed; the rate can be halted, slowed or accelerated, and adaptive styles can change. These factors include changes in the ethnic demographics of a community, prevailing sociopolitical attitudes and policies (e.g., segregation policies), economic conditions and practices (e.g., employment practices) and access to quality and higher education.

Furthermore, according to Szapocznik and Kurtines (1980), due to the fluctuating availability of opportunities and the prevalence of traditionally prescribed gender roles, the acculturation rate tends to vary between generations and across genders. Thus, the rate of acculturation is often faster for younger generations, and men tend to acculturate more quickly than women (see Figure 1).

The acculturation process is a key consideration in understanding the range of lifestyles inherent to various cultures. Various levels of assimilation, integration, rejection and deculturation can be observed in the various immigrant groups in the United States. As more first- and second-generation immigrants join the student population, educators need to be aware of the significance of culture and the enculturation process and their effects on students' behavior, development and learning needs.

In the next section, cultural relevance in family life education is discussed, and some initial recommendations are provided.

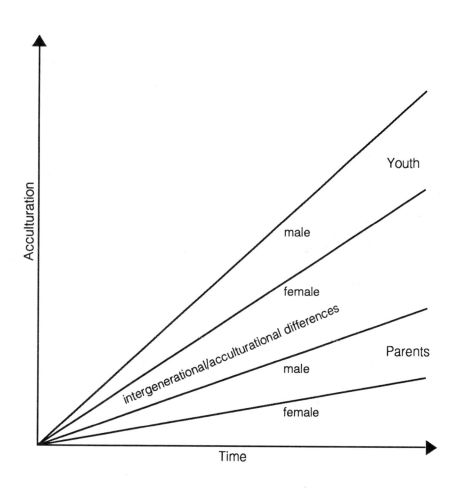

Figure 1. Theoretical model of acculturation depicting intergenerational and sex differences in acculturation.

Cultural Relevance in Family Life Education

F or the past few years, the trend in the family life education field has been to broaden the scope from lectures on puberty and reproductive anatomy to strengthening students' values and skills for living.

Current family life education is predicated on teaching useful "processes," whether a process for communication, a process for decision making, or a process for goal setting. These "processes" are taught by demonstrating, discussing and practicing situations that are "typical" to the learner. It is at this point that the teaching approach often breaks down, because the situations that are used to demonstrate or teach these "processes" are often not "typical" or even relevant to the bicultural or multicultural student.

These "processes" are most often taught in conformity to the norms of the dominant culture. Thus, they may not only fail to meet the needs of students from diverse cultural and ethnic backgrounds, but they may also cause confusion and create conflict between the students' cultural values and their desire to find a place in the youth culture.

The challenge of multiculturally-sensitive family life education is to help students identify their personal and cultural values, affirm the legitimacy and worth of their own "processes," and then help them manage the conflicts or issues that may arise from dealing with different sets of cultural norms and expectations.

To make family life curricula educationally and culturally relevant to students, educators need to understand the cultural implications of the topics and ideas being presented; use teaching materials that present a picture of life that reflects the reality of students' experiences; and address specific issues of cultural values, prejudice, stereotypes and intercultural conflicts.

Below are some specific recommendations to enhance the cultural relevance of family life education in the multicultural classroom:

- Acknowledge the need for culturally relevant teaching materials that reflect the diversity of the classroom.
- Get to know students individually in order to understand how they relate to their ethnic background.
- Investigate the traditions, beliefs and values of the various cultural groups represented by your students and reflected in your community.
- Review curricula and other resource materials to determine if they reflect the cultural diversity of the classroom.
- Use a student-centered approach, involving students in the development of teaching materials by having them define the situations and examples used in the classroom activities. This approach can be used as a basis for practicing communication, decision-making and goal-setting skills, respecting the cultural diversity of the classroom and meeting the needs of individual students, as well.

A Theory
of Self-Esteem

B ecause self-esteem is a key element in family life education, this section provides a brief yet tangible perspective on self-esteem and its relevance to the multicultural classroom.

Although educators do not unanimously agree on the definition or the dynamics of self-esteem, they do agree that positive self-esteem is important for all children if they are to grow up to be healthy, socially competent and productive adults. In addition to intellectual ability, one of the major contributors to children's academic achievement is their self-esteem. Academically successful students are likely to perceive themselves in primarily positive ways. Less successful students are more likely to perceive themselves in negative ways.

The relative strength of a child's self-esteem depends on the totality of a child's positive or negative experiences. The greater the number of positive experiences, the greater the likelihood of positive self-esteem. Unfortunately, children who experience racism, discrimination and poverty often have few positive experiences. These children need as many positive experiences as the educational system can provide.

Self-esteem is not a constant. It develops directly and indirectly through the child's social and personal experiences, and it can vary from one period of time to the next—and from one situation to another. Children may perceive themselves in a positive light within the home and in a negative light at school. A negative experience may have short- or long-term effects, depending on the significance attributed to the experience and its duration or frequency.

Negative self-esteem experiences in schools may not only impede children's ability and motivation to learn, but also result in their dropping out of school. Negative self-esteem experiences in schools may be a major contributor to the significantly high educational dropout rate for Hispanic and Black students. Because self-esteem is clearly important, educators must do what they can to provide *all* children with positive experiences that will engender in them positive outlooks toward themselves, their cultural and ethnic backgrounds and their educational pursuits.

The discussion and recommendations offered in this section address the cultural relevance of self-esteem within a theory developed by Harris Clemes and Reynold Bean (1981). We believe this theory offers a tangible framework that is applicable across cultures.

This framework was also used in the development of the Latino Family Life Education Curriculum Series published by ETR Associates/Network Publications. Sample lessons from the Latino Family Life Education Curriculum Series are provided in Special Sections.

Clemes and Bean have found that positive self-esteem can be attained when children experience positive feelings within four conditions. These four conditions are connectiveness, uniqueness, power and models. A brief explanation of each is provided below.

Connectiveness relates to the feelings children have when they gain satisfaction from significant associations and these associations are affirmed by others. Connectiveness includes:
- Identifying with a group of people.
- Feeling connected to a past or heritage.
- Feeling that you belong to something or someone.
- Feeling good about your relations or affiliations.
- Knowing that the people or things you are related to are considered in a positive light by others.
- Feeling important to others.

Uniqueness is the special sense of self children feel when they can acknowledge and respect qualities or attributes that make them special and different and when they receive respect and approval from others for these qualities. Uniqueness includes:

- Knowing that there is something special about yourself, in spite of recognizing that you are like many other people.
- Being aware that others think you are special.
- Being able to express yourself in individual ways.
- Respecting yourself as an individual.
- Enjoying the feeling of being different, without having to make others uncomfortable.

Power comes from having the resources, opportunity and capability to influence the circumstances of your life in important ways. Power includes:

- Feeling that you have influence and control over your life.
- Being able to use the skills you have in situations that require those skills.
- Feeling that you can make decisions and solve most of your problems.

Models are reference points that provide children with human, philosophical and operational examples that help them establish meaningful values, goals, ideals and personal standards. Models include:

- Knowing people you feel are worth emulating.
- Feeling confident that you can distinguish right from wrong and good from bad.
- Having values and beliefs that consistently help to guide and direct you.
- Feeling that you are working toward something, and knowing, more or less, where you are headed.
- Being able to make sense of your life surroundings.
- Being able to accomplish specific tasks in an organized manner.

Clemes and Bean believe that all children must experience these four conditions in as many situations as possible in order to develop and maintain a strong and pervasive self-esteem. They also believe that no single condition is more important than the others.

This overview of self-esteem is designed to help make self-esteem a more tangible construct as classroom activities are planned. In the following pages, recommendations and teaching

16

approaches are provided for each of the four conditions of self-esteem.

Connectiveness

For many students from diverse cultural backgrounds, a sense of connection to the extended family and identification with an ethnic group can be a strong source of self-esteem when those connections are respected by others. However, feelings of connectiveness with other people outside the family and ethnic group may be weakened by experiences of discrimination and feelings of being different.

Teachers can promote a sense of connectiveness in their students in several ways:

• Help students experience pride in the connection they feel with their friends, family, ethnic group, community and school.

• Promote a sense of connection among students by developing a climate of mutual respect.

• Foster mutual trust by using get-acquainted activities early in the course. Young people often isolate themselves in groups and cliques. They may have little interaction with other students outside their circle. Encourage students to look for similar interests and common values in classmates with whom they have not ordinarily communicated.

• Encourage cooperative learning. Affirm that cooperation, trust, mutual respect and interdependence are positive values in the classroom. Competition for grades or ranking in a classroom may create cultural conflict for many students. Research on learning styles (Aronson, 1978) revealed that Hispanic and Black students performed significantly better in cooperative learning situations than in competitive classrooms.

Uniqueness

Children derive a sense of uniqueness from feeling respected for characteristics that make them special and different. The key words here are *feeling respected*. For students from diverse cultural and ethnic backgrounds, feeling different can have adverse results if their cultural values and traditions are not shown positive regard.

Because many cultures tend to be interdependent rather than individualistic, family and ethnic culture may be vitally important in enhancing the students' sense of uniqueness.

Teachers can do several things to foster a sense of uniqueness in students in the multicultural classroom:

• Help students to see their culture as a source of values and pride.

• Reinforce the sense of uniqueness that comes from being a part of a family, a community and an ethnic group.

• Encourage students to see the influence of their culture on the positive aspects of who they are today.

• Recognize that individual uniqueness is not seen as a positive attribute in all cultures (e.g., in some cultures the individual should not stand out from the family), and help students recognize their uniqueness within that cultural or family framework.

Power

In order to possess a sense of power, children need to feel that they have ability to influence the events in their lives. They must be given the opportunity to learn a variety of skills, make significant choices and take responsibility for their actions.

As young people grow older, they encounter an increasing number of stressful situations. Clemes and Bean (1978) suggest that to maintain a sense of power, we must have a feeling of control. Students of all cultural backgrounds can strengthen their sense of personal power through improved decision-making and problem-solving skills, which can be augmented through classroom activities. In turn, as students learn to accept responsibility for their actions, they gain the opportunity for improved academic success.

With this in mind, there are several things educators can do to empower students:

• Help students identify their skills and abilities. Define these terms broadly. Include personality traits such as friendliness and a sense of humor, as they are sources of strength and power.

• Encourage students to give themselves positive messages to counteract the negative messages they receive.

• Direct students to develop control over thoughtless behavior. Help them understand how often they make decisions without thinking, and remind them that the decisions they make control what happens in their lives.

• Maintain high expectations for students. At the same time, provide clear and consistent standards of academic performance, so that students may live up to such expectations.

Models

Students from diverse cultural and ethnic backgrounds, and especially women, may be exposed to very few models of success whom they can emulate. Television and other media depict the success models of mainstream culture. There, success is most often defined in terms of money, glamour, political power, athletic prowess, etc. Very few of these models are members of diverse cultural and ethnic groups.

For this reason, it is important to help students acknowledge the strengths, talents and accomplishments of ethnic group members to reinforce pride and belief in their own abilities. Family life educators, in particular, should strive to present role models that encourage students to pursue their goals and become leaders of their communities.

Toward this end, teachers can:

• Emphasize visible, everyday role models. Parents, older siblings and other extended family members, as well as community leaders, can provide models of strength and accomplishment in situations relevant to students in the multicultural classroom.

• Counter the effects of TV's stereotypical treatment of minorities by challenging students to analyze the image and roles of different ethnic groups as they are portrayed in particular media projects.

• Bring leaders from diverse cultural and ethnic groups into the classroom for presentations.

• Discuss guidelines for classroom behavior and standards of academic performance with the students. Establish these guidelines as soon as possible in order to provide clear and consistent models for success in the classroom.

• Provide students with several decision-making models and discuss their relevance.

Guidelines for Teachers

The following recommendations are provided to help educators develop and teach family life education classes that are sensitive to and reflective of the cultural and ethnic diversity of their students and of society in general.

Since so much diversity exists within ethnic groups, no statements are made about the beliefs, attitudes or values of specific groups. Each teacher must explore the beliefs of individual students, the community and various groups within that community in order to represent the range of views that exist.

I. **General Statements**

    A. Get to know your students as individuals within their cultures.

    B. Since there is a wide range of values, beliefs and attitudes about family life education topics, assume that this range of views may be held by your students and their parents. This means leading classroom discussions that reflect diversity and modeling for students the willingness to hear ideas different than your own.

    C. To respect and reinforce the cultural perspective of each student, refer students to their parents or other significant adults for additional information and guidance.

D. Be sure that activities, discussions, films, written materials and guest speakers reflect the cultural and ethnic diversity of the students, the community and society in general. Involve advisory committees from diverse groups to help you select materials. (For additional curriculum guidelines, see Curriculum Guidelines for Multicultural Education in Special Sections.)

E. As part of your preparation for classroom discussions, assess how your own experiences, attitudes and values may impact the teaching process. Acknowledge your own attitudes and biases toward students from diverse cultural and ethnic backgrounds. Being aware of your personal biases can help you ensure that you present material in a balanced manner. (See Special Sections for Checking Out Your Biases.)

F. Be sensitive to the possibility that biases may exist among students and that parents may hold the same biases.

G. In helping students to overcome stereotypes, be aware that this process is quicker for some and slower for others.

II. **Recommendations for Specific Topics**
   A. Families
      1. Stress that there is no universally accepted definition of family. Definitions are influenced by individual experiences and cultural backgrounds.
      2. Present and validate families in a variety of forms, being sure to include the different family forms experienced by your students.
      3. Remember that parenting styles, forms of discipline and expressions of affection vary within various families according to their culture.
      4. Accentuate the family as a powerful source of support and advocacy.
      5. Increase students' awareness of the different roles and expectations they feel as a part of growing up male or

female in their families, their own ethnic culture and the larger culture in which they interact.

6. Facilitate students' recognition of intergenerational stress and value conflicts between family members that result from different rates of acculturation.

7. Facilitate communication between students and their parents to help overcome communication barriers due to acculturation.

8. Support the active involvement of parents as the primary sex educators of their children.

B. Self-Esteem

1. Recognize the importance of self-esteem as a factor in the achievement of academic and personal goals. Enhance students' sense of connectiveness, uniqueness, power and models.

2. Promote a sense of connection among students by developing a climate of mutual respect.

3. Encourage students to see themselves as unique and worthwhile individuals within the context of their cultural heritage.

4. Empower students by teaching personal responsibility and control over the direction of their lives.

5. Include visible role models of leadership and success. Encourage students to pursue their goals and become leaders of their community.

6. Be aware that many families consider the needs of the group over the needs of the individual. Reinforce the concept of power centered in family as well as in the individual.

C. Cultural Pride

1. Recognize that cultural pride is essential to the self-esteem and achievement of students in family life education classes.

2. Recognize that students live within the context of their cultural framework while also standing uniquely apart from it.

3. Help students recognize there are universal values that are commonly held by all cultures as well as values, traditions and beliefs unique to specific cultures.
4. Promote an understanding that although people from a distinct cultural and ethnic group generally hold certain values in common, particular families and individuals will differ from the norm.
5. Emphasize that culture changes in response to a continuously evolving environment, while at the same time providing consistency and values through time.
6. Create a climate of acceptance and affirmation of cultural differences.

D. Sex Roles
1. Define the term *sex roles*. Students may confuse this with sexual orientation. Point out that specific sex roles are influenced by one's culture.
2. Stress that one's cultural background can affect one's perception and experience of being male or female.

E. Relationships
1. When discussing dating with students, be aware that the correct age to begin dating and the range of acceptable dating activities may be influenced by the students' cultural background.
2. Remember that all people do not share the belief that the best way to communicate in relationships is by open discussion of feelings.

F. Skills for Change
1. Accentuate the students' ability to reconcile the many conflicting values and messages they may encounter in their lives. An important first step is to integrate the personal and cultural aspects of the individual.
2. Facilitate students' awareness of how their particular cultural heritage affects their ideas of family, interpersonal relationships and ethics. Encourage students to recognize the universal and unique values of each of

the cultures in which they operate and ways they can positively reconcile the differences.

3. Facilitate students' awareness of the presence of stereotypes in the society and development of skills to respond to stereotypes in an effective manner.
4. Enhance communication skills, enabling youth to communicate more effectively in each of the social spheres in which they function: peers, school, family and other relationships. Avoid setting rigid standards or models of communication that do not respect cultural norms and styles.
5. Develop students' awareness of the wide range of resources available for their use in effective decision making and achievement of their life goals.
6. Identify and develop skills of the natural leaders in the classroom and community who are respected by others and looked to for advice and guidance. Offer leadership training opportunities to develop skills in group facilitation and peer education so that natural leaders can take an even stronger role in the community.

G. Decision Making
   1. Acknowledge that the consequences of an action or decision may be seen differently by students based on their individual experiences and their cultural background.
   2. Stress that the best decision for the same situation may be different for each student, based on individual experience and cultural background.
   3. Remember that alternatives (options) in decision making are influenced by one's cultural background (e.g., resources, power, skills).
   4. When discussing consequences of a decision with students, examine how the decision might affect their families and their relationships with family members. Remember that the impact of decisions on the family and the concern students feel regarding this impact may be influenced by their cultural background.

5. Remember that the ability to implement decisions is influenced by one's cultural background (e.g., status in society, economic or educational levels, language, resources, etc.).
6. Promote decision-making skills that will enable students to explore an expanded range of opportunities, including career and educational opportunities. Encourage students to consider family values as well as individual strengths and desires when making decisions.

H. Reproductive Anatomy and Physiology, Adolescent Growth and Development
1. Help students recognize that males and females experience similar physical and emotional changes and concerns as they go through adolescence, regardless of their cultural background.
2. Dispel any myths related to anatomy, being sensitive that these myths may have been passed down by family members.
3. If topics such as hair care, make-up, beauty standards, etc., are discussed, include information and examples appropriate to students of different cultural backgrounds.
4. Keep in mind that the amount of discomfort or self-consciousness students feel in discussing these topics may be influenced by their cultural background.

I. Sexual Behavior and Orientation
1. Point out to students that one's culture helps develop one's values, beliefs and attitudes about sexual behavior and orientation.
2. Discuss with students the moral, religious, psychological, sociological and medical aspects of teenage sexual activity. Encourage students to discuss values with trusted adults within their family and cultural/ethnic group.
3. Help students dispel myths about human sexual behavior and orientation in a culturally sensitive manner.

4. When making a determination about language that can be used in the classroom, avoid the use of the term *proper*, since what is proper is subjectively defined. Tell students that medical terms will be taught to enable them to communicate knowledgeably and comfortably about sexuality. Allow students to ask questions in their own terminology until the corresponding medical term has been explained.

J. Parenting
  1. Emphasize that there are many successful styles of parenting and these are influenced by one's cultural background.
  2. In presenting information and leading discussions, remember that the perceived liabilities and benefits of parenthood are affected by one's cultural background.

K. Contraception
  1. Discuss various religious, moral and ethnic points of view about issues related to contraceptive use.
  2. Remember that self-esteem, sex-role conditioning and decision-making skills impact on contraceptive use and are influenced by culture.
  3. Be aware that some people consider the use of contraception a form of genocide.

L. Pregnancy Alternatives
  1. Discuss moral, religious, psychological, social, medical and legal aspects of each alternative. Be sure to include a variety of cultural views. Encourage students to discuss this issue with a trusted adult within their family and cultural/ethnic group.
  2. Remember that values and beliefs regarding each alternative can be influenced by cultural background.
  3. Do not assume or let students assume that all people of any particular group have a specific attitude or value related to any of the pregnancy alternatives.
  4. Do not assume that students in your class have not experienced pregnancy and its alternatives.

M. Sexually Transmitted Diseases
1. When making a determination about what language can be used to discuss sexually transmitted diseases, avoid the use of the term *proper*, since what is proper is a subjective interpretation. State that medical terms will be used in class. Allow students to ask questions in their own terminology until the corresponding medical term has been explained.
2. Do not assume that students have not experienced an STD.
3. Be familiar with neighborhood and community resources available and accessible to students.

Guidelines for School Districts and Decision Makers

T he following guidelines were developed in the broader context of improving educational opportunities for students in the multicultural classroom and are directed to school district administrators, state boards of education and the federal Department of Education.

I. To address the cultural diversity of students in family life education, **school districts** should:

A. Promote multiculturalism.
1. Hire staff that reflect the diversity of the school, the community and the nation. This includes actively recruiting multilingual as well as multicultural staff.
2. Develop and utilize classroom materials in the other languages that are represented in the classroom. Such materials should be developed independently and should reflect a range of cultural values and experiences. School districts should not rely on straight translations of existing materials.

B. Prepare varied types of family life education programs.
1. Develop long-term, comprehensive programs for kindergarten through twelfth grades.

2. Make short-term programs and workshops available for use during crucial decision-making periods, e.g., junior high. These programs can be used to supplement long-term programs or can serve as substitutes when funding is limited.

C. Organize an educational campaign for the local media.
　　1. Publicize information about family life and promote the values of respect and responsibility in individual, family and community relations through public service announcements, short TV spots and news articles.
　　2. Offer positive images of men and women from diverse cultural backgrounds while communicating about family life issues. Utilize popular media—including programming, movie scripts, and magazine articles—to promote positive images.

D. Extend teacher training opportunities.
　　1. Advocate increased federal and state funds for school districts to provide training in multicultural issues for teachers. If additional funding is unavailable, prioritize funding, using available resources to insure that teacher training is included in the current budget.
　　2. Educate teachers about new methods and goals of multicultural education, curriculum development, evaluation techniques and group facilitation skills. Promote the involvement of family members and other members of the community.

E. Evaluate programs regularly to assess their impact, and develop successful models, which can then be disseminated for the benefit of the wider community.
　　1. Use state-of-the-art methods of statistical analysis to assess long-term effects of programs on behavior, attitudes and skills.
　　2. Recognize that multicultural relevance in family life education benefits all students.
　　3. Obtain adequate funding by combining monies from the federal, state and county government sectors, as

well as from foundations and other private donors.

II. To address the educational needs of a multicultural student body within the United States, **state boards of education** and **federal decision makers** should:

A. Identify the development of strong multicultural education as a national priority.
　1. Recognize the important contributions that diverse cultural and ethnic groups can make to the educational process. View these groups as a vital resource to broaden children's knowledge of the diverse population of the United States.
　2. Require that curricula include strong cultural components that provide information about various ethnic backgrounds and experiences and promote acceptance and respect for diversity.

B. Mandate the development of culturally relevant family life education programs and curricula on a national scale.
　1. Require that family life programs incorporate a culturally relevant approach appropriate to the varied backgrounds of the populations being served.
　2. Appreciate the significance of family life education not only for its role in teaching communication and decision-making skills in the area of family health, but also in preparing students for future career and educational opportunities.
　3. Train new teachers from diverse ethnic and linguistic backgrounds to offer comprehensive and relevant family life education programs.
　4. Develop and advance teachers from diverse ethnic and linguistic backgrounds who already have a history of expertise in cross-cultural family life education.

C. Develop an institutional basis to address the broad context of family life education.
　1. Acknowledge that family life issues are affected by a

variety of factors—including opportunities for education, training, employment, political participation and representation. The development of opportunities for youth in all of these areas is required in order to effectively address family life issues.

2. Coordinate program development and implementation among all governmental departments concerned with education, employment and social welfare in order to address these related issues, particularly as they affect students from diverse cultural backgrounds.

3. Involve policy makers at all levels in order to implement programs effectively. While the local community must play a vital role in shaping the way programs are run, the needed financial backing and moral support to complete this task must come from federal, state and county governments.

D. Develop a humane, responsive policy regarding immigration and refugee status to address the needs of this growing segment of the U.S. population.

1. Appreciate the need for a consistent yet flexible policy to respond humanely to the needs of immigrants and refugees.

2. Recognize that immigrants and refugees are a unique population and that their needs will require ongoing attention in the coming decades. For example, family life education programs may need to address family crises that arise when children adapt more quickly than parents or grandparents to the new cultural environment. A responsive family life program could play a key role in promoting communication between generations in transition to a new culture.

E. Conduct comprehensive evaluative research on multicultural family life issues to fill in the gaps in data about specific groups. Respond to these findings with appropriate programs.

1. Advocate for funds for national studies of people from

diverse cultural backgrounds in the areas of health, education, employment and political participation, in order to assess the current conditions and potential needs.

2. Develop educational programs to address the issues identified by these studies. Collaborate with appropriate departments and other organizations to serve the diverse student population in the areas of need.

Special Sections

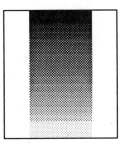

Checking Out Your Biases

These questions may help you identify ways you unintentionally show biases.

1. List five students you most like and feel most comfortable with and five for whom the reverse is true.
   a. Do these students have anything in common with each other, e.g., dress, language, behavior, cleanliness, manners, culture, ethnicity?
   b. Can you identify a bias that is indicated by their similarities?
2. Does the physical or seating arrangement in the room result in the better or brighter students being closer to you and having the best view of the blackboard?
3. Are privileges such as taking messages to the office or passing out papers and books unevenly distributed among students? Do smarter students or students from certain cultural/ethnic groups have more class privileges?
4. Do you spend more instructional time with one group of students than others?
5. Do you tend to wait longer for high achievers to respond to questions? Are you more impatient with low achievers and quicker to supply answers for them?

6. Do you tend to expect less from certain students? Are these children more likely to be economically deprived and minority members? Do they achieve less?
7. Do you tend to praise (with verbal and written comments) certain students more than others? Do these students tend to be from any particular economic, ethnic or cultural group?
8. Do certain students show signs of withdrawal, self-depreciation or aggression toward you or other students? Is this behavior more common among economically deprived and minority children?

Adapted with permission from *The Prejudice Book: Activities For The Classroom*, David A. Shiman. New York: Anti-Defamation League of B'nai B'rith, 1979.

Curriculum Guidelines for Multicultural Classrooms

As you review curricula, ask the following questions to determine if the curriculum is responsive to and reflective of the ethnic and cultural diversity of your students and society. Negative responses to questions may indicate areas where improvement is needed.

1. Have you ever evaluated your textbooks and other materials in terms of their treatment of different groups (e.g., ethnicity, sex, age, handicap, class)?
2. Do your instructional materials treat different groups honestly, realistically and sensitively?
3. Have you ever had the opportunity to study your students (e.g., their background, values, ways of thinking), with the aim of using this knowledge to improve instruction?
4. Do your instructional goals and strategies reflect the different cultures and learning styles of students in your class?
5. Do you think your curriculum helps students learn to function effectively in different cultures?
6. Do you think your curriculum contributes to strengthening students' senses of individual identity and helps them understand themselves better in light of their own heritage?
7. Does your curriculum include discussion of prejudice, dis-

crimination and exploitation and their effect on individuals and relationships?

8. Does your curriculum treat both positive and negative aspects of minority group experiences?
9. Does your curriculum help students examine similarities and differences both within and among different groups?
10. Do you help students distinguish facts from interpretations and opinions?
11. Do you spend sufficient time and effort dispelling misconceptions, stereotypes and prejudices that students appear to hold?
12. Do you introduce students to the experiences of persons of varying backgrounds and occupations within different groups?
13. Do you use materials written by and about members of different groups in your instruction?
14. Do you spend sufficient time helping students understand that different groups might perceive the same events or situations very differently?
15. Do you encourage and support students who wish to take action on social problems they have studied and are concerned about?

Adapted with permission from *Curriculum Guidelines for Multiethnic Education: Position Statement.* Arlington, VA: National Council for the Social Studies, 1976.

Sample Lessons

The four sample lessons provided in this section of the guide exemplify the use of the Clemes and Bean theory to develop curricula in multicultural classrooms. Although these lessons were developed with the specific needs of Latino students in mind, we believe the process is applicable to other cultures. All the sample lessons are from the *Latino Family Life Education Curriculum Series* (ETR Associates).

To provide a greater understanding of the four conditions of self-esteem as conceptualized by Clemes and Bean (1981), we offer the following examples:

The first lesson offers an example of helping students discover their **uniqueness**. It is from Lesson 1, "Differences," of the *Cultural Pride Curriculum Unit*.

The second lesson offers an example of identifying **power**. This is Lesson 4, "Personal Power and Confidence," also from the *Cultural Pride Curriculum Unit*.

The third lesson offers an example of **connectiveness**. This is Lesson 8, "Celebrating Family," of the *La Familia Curriculum Unit*.

The final lesson provides one process of identifying specific role **models**. This is Lesson 8, "Role Models," also from the *Cultural Pride Curriculum Unit*.

Please feel free to adapt these lessons to better serve the needs of your students.

Lesson 1
Differences

DICHO
▼▼▼▼▼

Cada cabeza es un mundo.

(Each person's mind is a world unto itself.)
This *dicho* addresses respect for the uniqueness
of each person's way of being.

Background and Rationale

The purpose of this lesson is to begin to acknowledge differences and to emphasize that differences make us special and unique. The activities are intended to reinforce positive feelings about cultural and individual identities. By utilizing the *papel en la pared* and displaying some of the work done, positive feelings about the student as an individual and as a member of the class will be reinforced. (See use of *papel en la pared* in the section on "How to Use The Curriculum.")

The lesson begins with definitions of **generalizations** and **stereotypes**. The "Potato Activity" introduces the students to the concepts of differences and uniqueness. With this activity students can begin to see that how we treat differences sometimes gets in the way of treating each other fairly. "Get to Know Your Partner" is an exercise that will help the students identify positive differences and unique characteristics in their classmates. The lesson ends in a positive way with the student completing the "My Partner Is Special" activity and writing one of the special characteristics of his or her partner on the *papel en la pared* for classroom display.

Teacher Preparation

Purchase a bag of potatoes, one potato for each student. Take three or four potatoes and cut holes in them or make them obviously different from the others. Obtain 4 or 5 large paper bags to put each group's potatoes in.

Prepare *papel en la pared* for the "My Partner Is Special" activity by cutting two large pieces of newsprint and labeling them. The newsprint should be large enough to accommodate the names and characteristics of all the students in the class. See example below:

My Partner Is Special

Partner's Name

Dora

One of the things that makes my partner special is...
...that she loves to read comic books in Spanish.

Time

Allow two 45-minute class periods for this lesson.

Outline of Activities

Activity	Materials Needed
Definition of terms	Glossary in student workbook
Potato Activity	One bag of potatoes
Get to Know Your Partner	"Get to Know Your Partner" student activity sheet
My Partner Is Special	*Papel en la pared*

Procedure

Potato Activity

I. Start this activity by introducing the student to the concept of **generalization**. Ask students if any of them know what it means to make generalizations. Provide the following definitions for clarification:

> A generalization is a statement or judgment that we make when we have only a limited amount of information about something. Making generalizations is a necessary part of thinking and reasoning. For example, we can make a generalization about moving cars: "A moving car can hurt us." We don't have to be run over by a car to arrive at that judgment. Generalizations are a way to categorize information so that we can make the right judgments about things. Although we make generalizations every day, we must be careful not to arrive at false or wrong generalizations about people. Making generalizations about people based on their race, culture, size, religion or any other characteristic that makes them different can keep us from relating to and learning from them.

To help students further understand, tell them that you are going to share a generalization with them and ask them if they agree with this statement: "All kids are alike." Encourage the students to state why this generalization is true or false. Other examples you could use are "all apples are red," "all older people have white hair," etc.

Tell students that another term that is important to know for this lesson is **stereotyping**.

> Stereotyping is something that happens when we assign characteristics to people because they are members of a group instead of getting information from experiences with them as individuals.

> Stereotypes are learned generalizations about people that have become fixed in our minds.

> Holding stereotypes about certain groups prevents us from thinking and feeling about members of those groups in new and different ways and blocks us from seeing them as unique, special human beings.

2. Roll potatoes out of a bag and ask each student to take one, examine it and take 1 or 2 minutes to learn about that potato, looking at the size, shape, color, texture and any other special characteristic that the potato may have. After 1 or 2 minutes have students form groups of 5 or 6. Distribute one large paper bag to each group and ask them to set the bags aside for the moment. Instruct students to describe their potatoes to their groups. A student may want to tell a short story about his or her potato. The story might focus on the physical traits of the potato; i.e., it has a bruise on its side because someone dropped it, or it has many eyes and can see in all directions. Encourage the students to get as creative in their descriptions as possible and find something that is unique and different about each potato.

    After the students have had an opportunity to describe their potatoes, ask them to put the potatoes back in their group's bag. Then ask the class if they would agree with the statement, "All potatoes are the same." Spend time processing both negative and positive responses (i.e., yes, one can see how people would think that all potatoes are the same if we grouped them all together but not if we take a more careful look at each one as an individual). Next, have one of the students in each group shake the bag of potatoes so the potatoes are mixed up and have each student find his or her original potato. Allow 2 more minutes for each student to tell how his or her potato was different from the others.

3. Have students return to the large group and discuss the following:
   • What are some of the differences you found in the potatoes?
   • Even though they are different, they also have a lot of things in common. What

do they have in common?

- Just like potatoes, people also have ways that they are different and ways that they are alike. In what ways are we alike? (We all have fears, hopes, feelings; we all need love.)
- We also have differences, those things that make us unique and special. In what ways are we different? (Color of our skin, language, dress, family customs, individual life experiences.)
- How were the potatoes that were very obviously different from the others described? What happens when there is more than one difference? (Sometimes the more layers of differences that exist, the harder it is to be accepted and treated fairly and equally.)

Conclude this part of the lesson by drawing an analogy between potatoes and people and by reiterating that a statement such as "they are all alike" is a generalization, and it usually means that the speaker has probably not taken the time or thought to get to know the person he or she is talking about.

Taking time to know about people means learning about how we are different and how we are alike. Acknowledging and accepting differences in ourselves and others increases our ability to understand each other.

Get to Know Your Partner

1. Tell students that this part of the lesson is intended to illustrate how each one of us is unique and different. Explain that the "Get to Know Your Partner" student activity sheet will help them do that in pairs. Divide class into pairs and give out the student activity sheet. Instruct students to take turns asking the questions and to write the answers in the space provided. They will have an opportunity to share their impressions with the rest of the class.

2. After all the students have had an opportunity to interview their partners, engage the group in a discussion about their discoveries.
   - What interesting thing did they learn about their partner?
   - What did they learn about themselves?
   - What did they learn about differences?
   - What did they think of the exercise?

My Partner is Special—*Papel en la Pared* Activity

1. Ask students to take a few moments to think about one thing that makes their partner special and unique.

2. Tape the *papel en la pared* on the wall and ask each student to take turns writing on it. Ask them to write their partner's name on the left side, and on the right side to finish the incomplete sentence: "One of the things that makes my partner special is..."

Summary

Emphasize that all of us are unique and different in our own way. Tell the students that the examples on the student activity sheet and the ones written on the *papel en la pared* are just a few examples of how we are different and unique. There are many other things that make us different and special.

Tell students that the lessons in the *Cultural Pride* curriculum will offer other opportunities to see how we are different, unique and special. Reiterate the *dicho* for this lesson— *"Cada cabeza es un mundo"*—meaning that everyone's mind is different and there is a world in each person's mind waiting to be discovered and respected.

Get to Know Your Partner

Ask your partner the following questions:

1. What is your favorite thing to do?

2. What do you like best about yourself?

3. What makes you feel the happiest?

4. What is it about yourself that makes you feel unique and different from others?

5. Do you identify yourself with a cultural group?
   If yes, which one?

6. If you don't identify yourself with a cultural group, what other group of people do you identify with?

7. What is different, unique or special about your group?

8. What is it about your culture or group that makes you feel proudest?

Lesson 4
Personal Power and Confidence

DICHO
▼▼▼▼▼

La ropa limpia no necesita jabón.

(Clean clothes don't need soap.)
This *dicho* means that there is no need to be overly concerned
about defending your position if you know you are right.

Background and Rationale

The story of Texcatlipoca (Tes-cah-tlee-po-cah) is an actual example of a cultural tradition—the **cuento**—used to express positive cultural values. This *cuento* is intended to affirm in the student a sense of personal power and confidence and the good feeling we get when we influence others.

The heroine of the story, Xochitl (So-cheel), is a young girl who acts confidently and honestly in spite of her fear of facing up to a force that appears to be much greater than she. The courage to respond as confidently and matter-of-factly as she did to Texcatlipoca is an indication of her own self-worth and assertiveness.

A secondary aim of this lesson is to present information via a culturally relevant vehicle, the *cuento*, in the context of Mexican lore. *Cuentos* are folk tales or legends that are passed on from generation to generation. We wish to reinforce that the Latino student's background offers relevant information about life that can affirm the student's worth and that this information is also worthy of sharing with others in our society so they can partake of its wisdom.

Teacher Preparation

Read story before class.

Write phonetic pronunciations and definitions of the following terms on the board:

Cuento (cu-en-toe) folk tales or legends that are passed on from generation to generation
Nahuatl (Na-wa-tl) language of the Aztecs
Texcatlipoca (Tes-cah-tlee-po-cah) smoking mirror in Nahuatl
Xochitl (So-cheel) flower in Nahuatl
Metate (Me-tah-teh) a stone for grinding corn in Nahuatl
Palomita (Pah-low-mee-tah) little dove

Time

Approximately one 45-minute class period.

Outline of Activities

Activity	Materials Needed
Read "Un Cuento: The Story of Texcatlipoca"	Student workbook
Discussion/ story summary	"Texcatlipoca" student activity sheet
Homework ideas	None

Procedure

Un Cuento (A Story)

1. Begin this lesson by explaining to students that the *cuento* of Texcatlipoca is a story based on an ancient Aztec legend that tells about the value of being secure in what we know is true even when someone is trying to overpower us. A *cuento* in the Latino cultures, as in many other cultures, is a traditional legend or story that is passed on from generation to generation. Sometimes these stories that are passed from generation to generation teach us about people's values; i.e., what they think is important in life, what they feel is right or what is wrong.

2. Read the *cuento* aloud to the students. Suggest that they close their eyes and try to imagine how the main character of the story, Xochitl, feels in the presence of Texcatlipoca. Encourage them to use their mind's eye to see the vivid colors of Texcatlipoca's costume and feel his power.

   After students have heard the story, discuss with them the notion of personal power and the importance of being able to express yourself.

   Point out Xochitl's strengths and how she demonstrated her own personal power by confidently stating her position in the midst of Texcatlipoca's anger.

3. When students have gained an understanding of the concepts in the story, have them fill out the "Texcatlipoca" student activity sheet.

   When students have completed their activity sheets, discuss the issues raised by the questions. Introduce the concept of personal power and explore with students some of the ways they can tap into their own personal power:
   a. being proud of accomplishments
   b. acting self-reliantly
   c. assuming responsibility easily
   d. tolerating frustration well
   e. feeling capable and confident in their relationships with others

Summary

Tell students that Texcatlipoca was considered to be one of the most powerful and most significant of the Aztec gods. The Aztecs' way of thinking about or understanding the universe was to a great degree a response to the fear of forces of nature which were unpredictable and brought with them extreme changes. The process of worship usually centered around offering presents, uttering prayers and performing symbolic acts to persuade the gods to act on behalf of the people. The ability of Texcatlipoca to transform himself from a person to a spirit, from the moon to the sun, and to change colors, forms and sizes was evidence of how powerful he seemed to the people that believed in him.

The diverse Latino cultures are rich with legends of ancient gods, heroes and heroines and advanced civilizations. Many *cuentos* such as this can be found in Latino communities. *Cuentos* or legends are stories that are handed down from generation to generation and often have their roots in something that really happened years ago. The Latino *cuentos* are a very significant way of passing knowledge and values from generation to generation. Legends and *cuentos* are constantly changing; they mix and blend with what is happening in a community and change as the community itself changes.

By listening to legends and *cuentos*, we can gain valuable information about our culture and what is important to the people of our culture.

Follow-Up Activity

Have students act out the story in class if time allows.

Homework Idea

Family Legends

Ask students to interview a family member and bring in other family legends that are passed on from the country of origin (e.g., *La Llorona, La Torcoata, The Troll Under the Bridge*, etc.). Many of these have morals, like *Aesop's Fables*, and these can be discussed as transmitters of culture or ways values get passed on from generation to generation.

Un Cuento
The Story of Texcatlipoca
(From Mexico)

The legend of Texcatlipoca is an ancient one that is perhaps based on fact, but the storyteller who first told it was famous for her lively imagination and inventiveness. As with all legends, the listener can decide what kind of truth it represents (and thus add to or take away from its power).

The story you are about to hear is about one of the most powerful gods of the Aztec people. Texcatlipoca was everywhere and knew what everyone was thinking and feeling.

He was so powerful that at night he was the moon, watching over the earth. During the day he was a god with human form. In his human form he looked as fierce as he was powerful. He had white spots on his forehead, nose and mouth, and he wore two pendants on each ear, one silver and one gold. On his lower lip he wore an emerald with a bright blue feather on it. His headdress was of pure gold and it circled around and ended on his ear, signifying that he could hear all pleas and supplications.

He wore an enormous medallion around his neck that served as a protective shield for his entire upper torso. In his right hand he carried four magical arrows, signifying his power to punish evil deeds. In his left hand he carried a round shield of polished gold that was also a blinding mirror. In this mirror all things could be seen. Tied to his feet were 20 golden bells and a deer's foot, symbolizing his agility. His cape was a black and white net adorned with fresh flowers of every color.

Texcatlipoca had great power over the world. The people in the villages feared him greatly and tried to make him happy in thousands of ways. They built special places at street corners and crossroads where he could sit and rest when he was roaming the earth overseeing his lands. Every five days the villagers, knowing his love for flowers, placed fresh bouquets on the resting stones on the streets and at the crossroads. On one of these days Xochitl was walking to her aunt's house to take the old woman some healing herbs for her rheumatism.

Xochitl, a young girl of 12, knew the legend of Texcatlipoca but she had never seen him. She had heard the people in the village say that Texcatlipoca had the power to appear and disappear in different forms and sizes. She wasn't even sure if she believed the stories. Her grandmother had always told her that she should only believe that which was true. Xochitl usually didn't give Texcatlipoca much thought.

51

Xochitl's aunt lived on the other side of the river, so Xochitl had to walk several miles and cross a bridge and several roads to get to her house. On the way she noticed the beautiful and colorful flowers at the resting places at the street corners and crossroads. She thought about her sick aunt and how her aunt loved fresh flowers. She knew her aunt would be happy to receive a bouquet, so she decided to exchange some of her fresh herbs for some of the flowers on one of Texcatlipoca's resting benches.

She gathered up the flowers in both hands, closed her eyes and took a deep breath, inhaling their sweet scent. She always smelled flowers in just this way; this was her special way of smelling flowers. She let the scent flow through her, swirling inside her mind and her being. When she opened her eyes, she saw someone standing before her. She had never seen, or even imagined, anything like him in her life.

When he spoke, his amazing voice echoed around her. It didn't sound like a human voice at all.

"What do you think you are doing?" he thundered.

Xochitl felt a little afraid, but her voice was clear and strong when she answered, "I am on my way to my aunt's house to pay her a visit and take her some herbs. I saw all these flowers and decided to take her some to cheer her up. These flowers are always here, and when they dry up they are thrown away and new ones are put in their place. Here, do you want to smell them? They are quite fresh and the scent is so sweet! I left some of my fresh herbs in exchange for the flowers I took. The herbs are especially good for rheumatism."

But before she had finished explaining, he roared in his mighty voice, "Aren't you afraid of me? Don't you know who I am? I am the mighty God of the Moon, Texcatlipoca! I can see everything and I know everything! I know what is in your heart!"

Xochitl answered, in a clear voice, "I am Xochitl and I come from the village of Nogales by the river. But I guess you already know that since you know all things."

Texcatlipoca was so furious at her insolence that he almost disappeared involuntarily. Even mighty beings such as he have trouble controlling their tempers.

But Xochitl did not notice his rage because she had just thought of something. "The people in my village say that you can heal all people who are sick. Is that right? Because if it is true, then I would like to ask you to heal my aunt's rheumatism. She is old and very wise, but sometimes she is in a bad mood because it hurts her to work in her garden or do her washing by the river..."

Xochitl was interrupted by Texcatlipoca, who by now was in such a rage that he turned into a lightning bolt and the earth shook with the force of his fury. Then he resumed human form, shaking the arrows and the brilliant gold shield he carried. The pendants in his ears and the bells on his feet clattered, and he roared at Xochitl, "Don't you know that I could strike you with my mighty shield and turn you into a *metate*? Aren't you afraid?"

Xochitl paused to collect her thoughts, and then she said, "Well, I have always heard that Texcatlipoca knows what is in everyone's heart and whether people have good or bad intentions. My grandmother always tells me that if I know who I am and my intentions are good, I don't have to be afraid. What do you think?"

And the rage left Texcatlipoca, because he knew that what Xochitl said was true. He sighed and sat down on the resting stone, taking his heavy shield off so he could sit more comfortably. Xochitl sat next to him and gave him some flowers, and he could see that her gift was made in friendship and not from fear. She admired his fabulous adornments and he explained their meaning. Then he said, "Where did you say your aunt lives?"

The girl turned to point in the direction of the road she was taking, and said, "In a little house just over the hill there. There are two chairs in front and a lovely garden." When she turned back, the god was gone.

Xochitl took her flowers and herbs and walked down the road toward her aunt's house. She got very excited thinking about the news she had to tell her aunt.

She thought to herself, "I am sure my aunt will say that I have a wonderful imagination, like she always does, and she will call me her *palomita* (little dove). And then she will say, 'Ay, *palomita*, what a wonderful storyteller you will be one day. Come here and let me braid your hair.'"

But Xochitl wouldn't mind, because she knew what had happened to her was true.

When Xochitl arrived at her aunt's house, she saw the most curious thing. It was her aunt, dancing out to greet her, her feet as light as air. She moved like a young girl!

"Ay, *palomita*, you'll never guess what happened!"

Texcatlipoca

1. Have you ever met someone who tried to make you believe he or she was much more powerful or important than you? How did you feel?

2. How did Xochitl respond to Texcatlipoca?

3. Why do you think Xochitl responded the way she did?

4. What do you think you can do to stand up for yourself in a positive way when someone tries to make you feel afraid or embarrassed?

5. What is something you have learned from an important person in your life who makes you feel strong and secure?

6. What are three things that you are proud of that you have accomplished recently?

This activity was inspired by: "The Story of Prince Krondak," *Self-Esteem: The Key to Your Child's Well-Being*, Harris Clemes and Reynold Bean.

Lesson 8
Role Models

DICHO
▼▼▼▼▼

Querer es poder.

(Where there's a will there's a way.)
This *dicho* means that with strong determination
almost anything is possible.

Background and Rationale

Having strong role models is one of the key ingredients in developing healthy self-esteem and cultural pride.

Unfortunately, the media and other mass influences in our society don't present culturally diverse models. This creates a gap for minority students who need help in identifying and acknowledging strong models in their own communities.

The stories of Romana Bañuelos, Anastacio "Don Tacho" Moreno and José Aponte have been adapted for that purpose. This lesson is designed to present students with successful Latina and Latino role models, each one presenting a different picture of success. The lesson includes a student activity sheet to help students identify role models within their own community.

Teacher Preparation

Read the three stories to determine which are more appropriate to your classroom needs. You can use one or a combination depending on your time constraints.

Time

Allow up to two 45-minute class periods for this lesson.

Outline of Activities

Activity	Materials Needed
Read stories	Three stories: Romana Bañuelos Anastacio Moreno José Aponte
Discussion	None
Identify role models	"My Role Model" student activity sheet

Procedure

Stories

Romana Bañuelos

1. Tell students that poverty can be a major barrier for many people wanting to have a career and become successful. However, some people have overcome seemingly insurmountable problems. Explain that Romana Bañuelos is one of those people and they will be hearing a story about her.

2. Write the following statements on the board as you tell the story:
   • Born in Mexico.
   • Divorced, with two children, at 18.
   • Said "I can make it."
   • Came to the United States and worked in a laundry in Texas for a dollar a day.
   • Said "I can do better."
   • Moved her family to California with $7 in her pocket.
   • Saved $400 and bought a tortilla factory.
   • Said "I can be a success."
   • Built a one-room tortilla factory into a $5-million-a-year business.
   • Established the first bank to serve the East Los Angeles Mexican-American community after being told, "You are not qualified. You can't make it."
   • Appointed by the president to be the 34th Treasurer of the United States.

Anastacio "Don Tacho" Moreno

1. Ask students for their ideas on what makes a person successful. After the students have an opportunity to share what they think makes a person successful, explain that being financially successful is just one example of success. Other examples may be having a special way of talking with people, being respected in your community or neighborhood (for helping others), being considered a helpful neighbor or a wise person who gives good advice, or having some special knowledge about things such as health, gardening, cooking, animals, sports, cars, etc. Being successful can also mean having a simple and happy life.

   Explain that Anastacio Moreno was one of those people who had a simple and happy life. He did not have a lot of money but people in his neighborhood respected him for his special knowledge about animals and his kind attitude toward others, including the children in the neighborhood.

2. Write the following statements on the board as you tell the story:
   - Born in the USA of Colombian parents. Completed 6 years of school.
   - Developed a love for and interest in animals at an early age. Believed to have a special gift for healing animals.
   - Married for 50 years to Doña Rita. Raised two boys and helped them go to college and technical school.
   - Lived in the same neighborhood for most of his life.
   - Worked as a school janitor for 30 years at the same school.
   - Neighbors relied on him to help when their pets were sick.
   - Known in the neighborhood as *Don Tacho, el de los pichones* (Don Tacho, the one with the pigeons).
   - Doña Rita died when Don Tacho was 79.
   - His sons and his neighbors pulled together and helped him take care of himself until he died at age 84.
   - Anastacio "Don Tacho" Moreno, a well respected member of his *barrio* and his community. Special because he was good with animals and kind to his neighbors.
   - Believed in himself.

José Aponte

1. Start the story about José Aponte with the same approach that was used in introducing Mrs. Bañuelos' and Don Tacho's stories. After emphasizing to students that there are different ways of being successful, tell students that José Aponte is a Puerto Rican librarian who is also a community leader and is dedicated to helping Latinos become more educated. His story is provided to offer yet another example that there are many ways of being successful.

2. Write the following statements on the board as you tell the story:
   - José Aponte, Puerto Rican, married, two children.
   - Born in New York City.
   - Raised by a single working mother in South Bronx, New York.
   - José's mother was one of the first Spanish-speaking librarians in the country.
   - Spent his early childhood in New York City in the South Bronx in an area called Hell's Kitchen.
   - Had his first job when he was eight years old, reading stories to children at the library for 25 cents a story.
   - Successful in school and had good grades.
   - In 1967 he felt bored in high school and decided to drop out to go to work in the agricultural fields in Florida.
   - Worked 6 months for $3.00 a day and then realized the importance of staying in school and asked his mother for help.
   - His mother sent him money for his bus ticket back to New York.

- Returned to high school and graduated in 1969.
- Won several scholarships and went to college. Graduated from college and attended graduate school where he earned a master's degree in library science.
- Two most influential people in his life are his mother and his wife.
- Most important things in his life are his family, his spiritual well-being, his health and his commitment to his people.
- José Aponte defines success as "the ability to work at what I enjoy and serve my people."

Discussion

Discuss student reactions to the stories using the following questions to frame and direct the discussion:

- What or who do they think contributed to Mrs. Bañuelos', Don Tacho's or José Aponte's belief in themselves?
- How do they define success?
- What do you think is the most important factor needed in order to succeed in life?
- What about their family or themselves convinces them that they can be a success in life?

Role Models

1. As the teacher, tell students about your most significant role model, someone you looked up to and tried to be like. Be sure to tell them how you know the person. Was he or she a member of your family, a friend, a teacher? Why did you look up to her or him? What do you think you learned from her or him?

2. Have students think of someone they admire and write about their most significant role model. Explain to students that this person can be someone they know personally, a friend or family member, or someone they look up to who appears on TV or in a book. (It can also be someone in their family who lived in the past but whom they have always heard about, like a great-grandmother or grandfather.)

3. Direct students to their workbooks and ask them to write their responses to the questions in a paragraph. Encourage them to use the entire page.

Summary

Close this lesson by telling students that having role models, people in our lives that we admire, is important. As we grow and develop our life goals we look to people who have been important to us and see how we can use what they've done as examples of how to live. Encourage students to look in their families, *barrios* and communities for people whom they like and admire and ask themselves, "What can I learn from this person? What would I do differently? What would I do the same?"

Romana Bañuelos

Romana Bañuelos was born in Mexico. She was married as a teenager and had two children. She was divorced at 18. Despite the obvious problem of being a young divorced woman with two children, Romana Bañuelos said to herself, "I can make it."

She immigrated to the United States and lived in Texas where she worked in a laundry for one dollar a day. As she struggled with poverty trying to care for her children, Mrs. Bañuelos told herself, "I can do better."

One day she moved to California with only $7.00 in her pocket. She worked, took care of her children and saved $400. With her savings Mrs. Bañuelos bought a tortilla factory in Los Angeles. She said to herself, "I can have success." Over a period of years, Romana Bañuelos' one-room tortilla factory became a $5-million-a-year business.

Mrs. Bañuelos wanted to serve the East Los Angeles Mexican-American community where she lived and worked. When she tried to establish a bank that would benefit her community, she was told that she wasn't qualified and should forget her dream—give up her goal. "You can't make it," she was told. Despite discouragement, Romana Bañuelos did establish the bank.

Later, Mrs. Bañuelos was appointed the 34th Treasurer of the United States.

Adapted from: *How to Be Successful in Less Than Ten Minutes a Day.* B. David Brooks, PhD and Robert C. Paull, PhD. Pasadena, CA: Thomas Jefferson Research Center, 1984.

Anastacio "Don Tacho" Moreno

Anastacio Moreno, "Don Tacho" as he was known in his *barrio*, lived a full life. He was born in the United States of Colombian parents in 1901. He was the eldest son of a family of eight children.

One of the things that Anastacio loved to do as a young boy was take care of the family animals—pigeons, chickens, goats and rabbits.

Because his parents were very poor, he dropped out of the sixth grade to help support his younger brothers and sisters. He worked at different kinds of low paying and seasonal jobs for many years and he often wished he had more education. During the Great Depression it was hard to get work; it was even harder if you had no education.

Like many Latino men during World War II, Anastacio fought for his country. He was proud of that. When he came back from Germany, what he wanted more than anything was to settle down and get a steady job.

As soon as he returned, Anastacio got a job as a janitor at the local school in the same neighborhood where he spent most of his childhood—*Barrio Anita*.

Later that year he met Rita Muñoz at the weekly dance in the plaza across the street from the church. They were married the following year. They built a small adobe house on a corner lot in *Barrio Anita*. In that same *barrio*, Anastacio and Rita raised two boys and helped them go to college and technical school—something Anastacio wished he had been able to do.

What Anastacio loved most about his life during those years was his family, his job, his *barrio* and his animals.

He was an animal lover and people used to say he had the gift of healing animals. Anastacio kept all kinds of animals in his back yard—pigeons, chickens, goats and rabbits. Later he also had dogs and cats and a parrot he called Cuca. His house soon became the center of the *barrio*.

Every day in the late afternoon before dinner, the neighborhood children came to help him feed his animals. And everyday, after work, hundreds of pigeons would flock to the front of his house to be fed. It was plain to see that Anastacio was a very special person, because the animals, the birds and the children trusted him and loved him.

As the years went by, families with pets in the neighborhood relied on him to help with their sick or injured animals. One summer when Doña Pelona's prized rooster, Kiko, was run over by the UPS truck, no one thought the rooster would live. Doña Pelona brought the beautiful black and red bird over to Don Tacho's house wrapped up in a towel like a baby. The rooster was weak and badly injured. Although he recuperated slowly, he was out dodging cars in the streets again by the time school started.

The children and the families in his neighborhood all loved Anastacio. At first they called him Tacho, short for Anastacio, and as he got older and became more respected, they called him "Don Tacho." The *barrio* mothers and grandmothers always called him *Don Tacho, el de los pichones* (Don Tacho, the one with the pigeons).

Don Tacho lived a simple life. He lived, worked, raised his family and died in the same *barrio*.

Doña Rita died when Don Tacho was 79 years old. Although he lived alone until he died at age 84, his neighbors and sons watched over him, helped him with his groceries and continued asking for his advice about sick pets and injured pigeons.

Don Tacho was a respected member of his *barrio* and his community. He believed in himself, gave of himself and in return, accepted what life had to give him.

José Aponte

José Aponte is known in his community as "the lively librarian." José is Puerto Rican. He was born and raised in New York City. His job, he says, is to build bridges from the community to the library. He hopes that someday all people in this country will feel at home at the library and take advantage of the many treasures that can be found there.

José was born in New York City in the South Bronx in an area called Hell's Kitchen. He and his sister were raised by their single mother in the 1960s, a time of great change for Latinos and other minorities in this country. José's mother was one of the first Spanish-speaking librarians in this country.

José earned his first wages at the library when he was 8 years old. Every day after school José and his sister Gloria would ride the bus to the library where their mother worked. There José would read stories to the children for 25 cents a story.

One of the hardest things that José had to face when he was a young boy was discrimination at his school. In 1961, José's mother moved her children to a school that had previously been attended only by white children. When Gloria and José arrived at the school, they called José "Black Sambo" and mistreated his sister. José remembers that what got him through those difficult years in school was his mother's love and understanding and his pride in being Puerto Rican. José's mother always taught her children to be proud of their rich culture and heritage.

José always had good grades in school but sometimes he felt bored. When he was 16 years old he was bored in high school and decided to drop out and go work in the fields in Florida. He worked 6 months. In the fields he earned $3.00 a day; he had to pay $1.00 a day for food and $1.00 a day for his room. That left him with only $1.00 a day for all his other expenses. He was very discouraged. He wanted to go home, and he didn't even have the fare for his bus ticket back to New York. High school never looked so good. He didn't want to ask his mother for money because he was embarrassed, as she had advised him not to go. He finally swallowed his pride and called his mother for help. His mother told him she was sorry things didn't work out like he had wanted them to but that she was glad that he had learned from the experience. She agreed to send him the exact amount for the bus ticket and he agreed that he would work and pay her back as soon as he could.

José returned to high school and graduated in 1969. He won several scholarships and continued his education until he earned a master's degree in library science.

José is married now and is head of his own library. Reading stories to children is still one of his favorite things to do. He considers his mother and his wife the two most influential people in his life. When you ask José , "What are the most important things in your life?" he answers quickly and confidently, "My family, definitely, my spiritual well-being, my health, and my people."

My Role Model

1. Write a paragraph about the person you most admire (If you like, you can write this person's name; if not, you can keep it a secret and just describe the person and why you look up to him or her.)

2. Using the space below, write more about your favorite role model. How do you know this person? How did you meet? Is this person a part of your family, neighborhood, church? Is it a friend, a TV hero or heroine? An ancestor that goes back generations?

3. Why do you admire this person?

4. What is the most significant thing or things that you have learned from this person?

5. Name one quality that this person has that you would like to have.

6. What more would you like to learn from this person?

Lesson 8
Celebrating Family

DICHO
▼▼▼▼▼

Amor con amor se paga.

(Love is repaid by love.)

This *dicho* states that if you give love, you will receive love.
It was taken from the thoughts and writing
of José Martí, a dedicated Cuban leader who fought
for Cuban independence from Spain.

Background and Rationale

The final lesson of *La Familia* ends in celebration of the family. The activities provided in this lesson are intended to bring closure to the unit by encouraging students to acknowledge what is special about their families. Students will have an opportunity to do this by completing the writing activity in their workbooks, sharing with their class-mates and finally, by painting a mural that illustrates what celebrating family means to them.

We encourage the teacher to bring refreshments and end this unit with a *fiesta*. This celebration could also be a good opportunity to invite parents to class to share in celebrating *La Familia.*

Teacher Preparation

At least a week before the final lesson, decide with students the kind of celebration there is to be. Plan for foods and beverages and other *fiesta* ideas. Contact family members as appropriate. Prepare as many sheets of *papel en la pared* as needed for murals. Obtain tempera paints, colored markers, tape, scissors, etc.

Time

Allow up to two 45-minute class periods for this lesson.

Outline of Activities

Activity	Materials Needed
"What Makes My Family Special to Me?"	"What Makes My Family Special to Me?" student activity sheet
Celebrate Family Mural	*Papel en la pared,* tempera paints, markers, other appropriate materials for mural painting.

Procedure

What Makes My Family Special to Me?

1. Tell students that this activity is part of the celebration and closing of *La Familia* unit and that it is an opportunity for students to acknowledge some of their families' special qualities.

   Acknowledge that sometimes we are upset with our families and that it is hard to see their positive sides. The object of this last exercise is for students to spend time thinking about what they really like and find positive about their families.

2. Direct students to their workbooks and ask them to look at the student activity sheet and answer the question, "What makes my family special to me?" Tell students to list 5 specific actions, qualities, beliefs or practices that they value or like in their families. Ask students to describe what it is about the special family quality that they admire that gives them enjoyment. For example, a student who enjoys weekends with his family might say that he particularly likes playing softball with his aunts, uncles and cousins when they go to the park on Sundays. Have students write an essay using the first question as the topic and including the five qualities they listed.

   Encourage students to take their student activity sheets or essays home to share with their family members. Tell students that often other family members don't realize how important or enjoyable certain family times can be and this is a good opportunity to show them how much they are appreciated.

   Tell students they will have an opportunity to use some of the good qualities they identified in their families in the final exercise of this lesson.

Celebrate Family Mural

1. Tell students that to end the unit on *La Familia*, they will have an opportunity to create a mural. The title of the mural is "Celebrate Family." Divide class into groups of five and ask them to spend about five or ten minutes discussing how they could paint a mural celebrating family. Students can draw or paint the mural in any way they want as long as it expresses a feeling of celebration of family. Encourage them to go back to Lesson 7 and look through the traditions and celebrations and incorporate those ideas, as well as some of the good qualities they identified in the "What Makes My Family Special to Me?" activity. Instruct each group to take one of the *papeles en la pared* and start their murals. Each group's goal should be to have fun,

be creative and in the spirit of group cooperation, create a mural that will reflect the most positive qualities, traditions and activities that celebrate the family. Tell students that they have 20 minutes to create the mural. Advise the groups when they have 5 minutes left.

2. After students have completed the murals, tape murals to the walls and ask each group to explain them to their classmates. Encourage other students to ask questions. Some questions may be: why a certain tradition was chosen, how the group feels about their creation, what features were put in and why.

Leave the murals up two or three weeks for the class to enjoy.

Summary

Tell students that this is the final lesson of *La Familia* and that its purpose was to help students further explore the positive family traits that contribute to their sense of family solidarity and pride. Encourage them to continue in their exploration and affirmation of who they are in the context of their families and culture.

What Makes My Family Special To Me?

1. _____

2. _____

3. _____

4. _____

5. _____

Selected Resources

Curricula

America's Women of Color: Integrating Cultural Diversity into Non-Sex-Biased Curricula. Secondary Curriculum Guide. Women's Education Equity Act Program (ED), Washington, DC. Saint Paul, MI: Saint Paul Public Schools, 1982.

La Comunicación: Curriculum Unit with *Student Workbook.* Latino Family Life Education Curriculum Series. Grades 5-8. Gene T. Chávez. Santa Cruz, CA: ETR Associates, 1989.

Cultural Pride: Curriculum Unit with *Student Workbook.* Latino Family Life Education Curriculum Series. Grades 5-8. Ana Consuelo Matiella. Santa Cruz, CA: ETR Associates, 1988.

Culture and Children. Gayle Brown et. al. Austin: Texas State Department of Human Resources, 1984.

Entering Adulthood: Coping with Sexual Pressures. Grades 9-12. Contemporary Health Series. Nancy Abbey and Elizabeth Raptis Picco. Santa Cruz, CA: ETR Associates, 1989.

Ethnic Pride: Explorations into Your Ethnic Heritage. Greta Barclay Lipson and Jane A. Romatowski. Carthage, IL: Good Apple, Inc., 1983.

La Familia: Curriculum Unit with *Student Workbook.* Latino Family Life Education Curriculum Series. Grades 5-8. Ana Consuelo Matiella. Santa Cruz, CA: ETR Associates, 1988.

Family Life Education Curricula. La Clinica de la Raza. Oakland, CA: 1985.

Family Life Education: Curriculum Guide. Revised edition. Grades 7-12. Edited by Steven Bignell. Santa Cruz, CA: ETR Associates, 1984.

Life Planning Education: A Youth Development Program. Center for Population Options. Washington, DC: March, 1985.

Love, Sex and Marriage: A Jewish View. Rabbi Roland Gittelsohn. New York: Union of American Hebrew Congregations, 1980.

The Multicultural Caterpillar: Children's Activities in Cultural Awareness. Grades K-3. Ana Consuelo Matiella. Santa Cruz, CA: ETR Associates, 1990.

Open Minds to Equality: A Sourcebook of Learning Activities to Promote Race, Sex, Class and Age Equality. Nancy Schniedewind and Ellen Davidson. Englewood Cliffs, NJ: Prentice-Hall, 1983.

The Prejudice Book: Activities for the Classroom. David A Shiman. New York: Anti-Defmation League of B'nai B'rith, 1979.

Project Pride: Elementary Attitudes and Skills for Substance Abuse Prevention. Paula Randall and Sherri Guendelsburger Romanoski. Tucson, AR: CODAC Behavioral Health Services, 1984. Spanish adaptation by Ana Matiella. Tuscon, AR: Hispanic Information Design, 1986.

La Sexualidad: Curriculum Unit with *Student Workbook.* Latino Family Life Education Curriculum Series. Grades 5-8. Elizabeth Raptis Picco. Santa Cruz, CA: ETR Associates, 1990.

Sexuality Education: A Curriculum for Adolescents. Pamela M. Wilson and Douglas Kirby. Santa Cruz, CA: ETR Associates, 1984.

Super Me Super You: A Bilingual Activity Book for Young Children. U.S. Department of Health, Education and Welfare. Rockville,

MD: 1985. Available from Superintendent of Documents, U.S. Government Printing Office, Washington, D.C.

We Are a Family: Children's Activities in Family Living. Grades K-3. Ana Consuelo Matiella. Santa Cruz, CA: ETR Associates, 1990.

Journal Articles and Papers

"Black Teenage Pregnancy: A Challenge to Educators." Joyce A. Ladner. *Urban League Review* 11, no. 2 (Summer-Winter 1987-88): 236-244.

"A Comprehensive Life-Planning Model for Black Adolescents." Courtland Lee and Susan Simmons. *School Counselor* 36, no.1 (September 1988): 5-10.

"Cooperative Learning in the Urban Classroom." *ERIC/CUE Digest* 30. (1986).

"Family Life Education for Young Inner-City Teens: Identifying Needs." *Journal of Youth and Adolescence* 16, no.4 (August 1987): 261-377.

"The Great Learning Enterprise of the Four Worlds Development Project." Richard Fiordo. *Journal of American Indian Education* 27, no. 3 (May 1988): 24-34. Describes a curriculum based on a project to eliminate Native American substance abuse through traditional Native American values.

"Multicultural Education." Ohio State University. *Theory into Practice* 23, no. 2 (Spring 1984). Special issue.

"Multicultural Education: A Challenge for Teachers." Eldering van den Berg and Ed Lotty et. al. Paper presented at a Conference on Multicultural Education and Teacher Training, Amersfoort, The Netherlands, September 27-30, 1982.

Books and Pamphlets

Children's Ethnic Socialization: Pluralism and Development. Jean S. Phinney and Mary Jane Rotheram, editors. Newbury Park, CA: Sage Publications, 1987.

Come Closer Around the Fire: Using Tribal Legends, Myths and

Stories in Preventing Drug Abuse. Center for Multicultural Awareness. Arlington, VA: 1978.

Culture in the Classroom: A Cultural Enlightenment Manual for Educators. Laura Loridas. Wayne County Intermediate School District, Lansing, MI: Michigan State Department of Education, 1988.

Differences: A Bridge or a Wall. Dan Willis with Jos Meyer. Citizen Involvement Training Program, School of Education, University of Massachusetts, 1983.

Diversity in the Classroom: A Multicultural Approach to the Education of Young Children. Frances E. Kendall. (Teachers College, Columbia University) New York: Teachers College Press, 1983.

Education in Sexuality for Christians: Guidelines for Discussion and Planning. United States Catholic Conference. Washington, DC: 1981.

Educational Materials for Multicultural Education. Anti-Defamation League of B'Nai B'rith. New York: 1989.

Guide for Multicultural Education: Content and Context. California State Department of Education. Sacramento: 1977.

Guide to Multicultural Resources, 1987 Edition. Charles A. Taylor Madison, WI: Praxis Publications, 1987.

Guidelines for Selection of Bias-Free Textbooks and Storybooks. The Council on Interracial Books for Children, New York.

Helping Kids Learn Multi-Cultural Concepts: A Handbook of Strategies. Michael G. Pasternak. Champaign, IL: Research Press Company, 1979.

Human Relations Materials for the School. The Anti-Defamation League of B'Nai B'rith. New York: 1989.

Intercultural Skills for Multicultural Societies. Carly H. Dodd and Frank F. Montalvo. Washington, DC: SIETAR International, 1987.

Latino Families in the United States. A Resourcebook for Family Life Education and *Las Familias Latinas en los Estados Unidos.*

Recursos para la Capacitacion Familar. Sally J. Andrade, editor. New York: Planned Parenthood Foundation, 1983.

A Nation for Families: Family Life Education in Public Schools. A Handbook of Realities, Recommendations and Resources for Educators, Administrators and Community Leaders. William G. Sheek. Palo Alto, CA: William and Flora Hewlett Foundation, 1984.

Razalogia: Community Learning for a New Society. Roberto Vargas and Samuel C. Martinez. Oakland, CA: Razagente Associates, 1984.

Teaching and Learning in a Diverse World: Multicultural Education for Young Children. Patricia G. Ramsey. (Teachers College, Columbia University) New York: Teachers College Press, 1987.

Where to Find Data About Adolescents and Young Adults: A Guide to Sources. Children's Defense Fund. Washington, DC: Adolescent Pregnancy Prevention Clearinghouse, 1989.

Reports

"And Justice for All: The NEA Executive Committee Study Group Reports on Ethnic Minority Concerns." National Education Association. Washington, DC: 1987.

"Bridging the Challenging Years: Tips for Working with American Indian Teenagers". Office of Educational Research and Improvement. Washington, DC: 1988.

"Curriculum Guidelines for Multiethnic Education: Position Statement." National Council for the Social Studies, New York: Anti-Defamation League of B'nai B'rith, 1976.

"Emphasis on Latin American Cultures," Disadvantaged Pupil Program Fund. Evaluation Report. Department of Research and Analysis, Cleveland Public Schools. Cleveland, OH: 1983.

"Junior High Migrant Student Services: A Compendium." (State University of New York) Oneonta, NY: College at Oneonta, 1985.

"Use of the Semantic Differential in Teaching About Minority Group Families." Linda Padou Burkett. Minnesota: 1985.

References

Aronson, E. 1978. *The jigsaw classroom.* Beverly Hills, CA: Sage Publications, Inc.

Clemes, H. and Bean, R. 1981. *Self-esteem: The key to your child's well-being.* New York: G.P. Putnam's Sons.

Fitzpatrick, J. P. and Gurack, D. J. 1979. *Hispanic intermarriage in New York City: 1975.* New York: Fordham University Hispanic Research Center.

Ford Foundation. 1984. *Hispanic: Changes and opportunities.* New York: Ford Foundation.

Jaffe, A. J., Cullen, R. M. and Boswell, T. D. 1980. *The changing demography of Spanish Americans.* New York: Academic Press.

Mead, M. 1970. *Culture and commitment: A study of the generation gap.* Garden City, NY: Doubleday.

Social Science Research Council Summer Seminar. 1954. Acculturation: An exploratory formulation. *American Anthropologist* 56:973-1002.

Stonequist, E. V. 1935. The problem of the marginal man. *American Journal of Sociology* 41:1-12.

Contributors

Nancy Abbey is a nationally known family life and sexuality educator with many years of experience working with youth from diverse ethnic groups. As a teacher of a program for school-age mothers and fathers and as a community health educator, Ms. Abbey has spent much of her professional life in direct contact with young people and their struggle for individuality and connection. During her years at ETR, she has been closely involved with the development of curriculum and classroom materials that help students to be seen both as individuals and as members of various cultures. Ms. Abbey worked with Dr. Manuel Casas and Dr. Claire Brindis in collaboration with an expert panel of educators to establish guidelines and materials for multiculturally relevant and appropriate family life and sexuality education.

Claire Brindis, DrPH, is Co-Director for the Center for Reproductive Health Policy Research, Institute for Health Policy Studies, University of California, San Francisco. She coordinates research, technical assistance and dissemination activities within the Center. Her interests in the field of reproductive health include adolescent pregnancy and family life education, high risk-taking behaviors among youth, and cost-benefit analyses within the field of family planning. Her current research endeavors include the evaluation of 9 school-based health centers in California who provide primary care services to underserved populations, policy analysis in the field of teenage pregnancy and pregnancy prevention, and evaluating interventions in the field of substance abuse.

J. Manuel Casas, PhD, was born in Chihuahua, Mexico. He completed his undergraduate work in political science at the University of California, Berkeley, and he received his MA and PhD in counseling psychology from Stanford University. He is a member of the editorial board for the *Journal of Multicultural Counseling and Development.* Dr. Casas has published and lectured extensively in the areas of his research specialization: the dynamics of the Hispanic family and counseling and educational needs of families from diverse ethnic populations. He is an Associate Professor of Counseling Psychology, Department of Education, University of California, Santa Barbara.

Ana Consuelo Matiella is Editor and Staff Writer for ETR Associates/Network Publications in Santa Cruz, CA. She is the series editor for ETR Associates' Latino Family Life Education Curriculum Series and has written two of the units in the series: *Cultural Pride* and *La Familia* (1988). She has authored two activity books for children, *The Multicultural Caterpillar* and *We Are a Family* (1990, ETR Associates.) Additionally, Ms.

Matiella is in charge of materials development for the California AIDS Clearinghouse. One of her particular interests and areas of expertise is fotonovela production.

Ms. Matiella is bilingual and bicultural and was raised on the border of the United States and Mexico by a clan of Mexicans and Spaniards.